Drew and Drake

Mary Elizabeth Salzmann

Consulting Editor, Diane Craig, M.A./Reading Specialist

ABDO
Publishing Company

Published by ABDO Publishing Company, 4940 Viking Drive, Edina, Minnesota 55435.

Printed in the United States.

Credits ·
Edited by: Pam Price
Curriculum Coordinator: Nancy Tuminelly
Cover and Interior Design and Production: Mighty Media
Child Photography: Steven Wewerka, Wewerka Photography
Photo Credits: AbleStock, John Foxx, Photodisc

Library of Congress Cataloging-in-Publication Data

Salzmann, Mary Elizabeth, 1968-
    Drew and Drake / Mary Elizabeth Salzmann.
        p. cm. -- (First sounds)
    Includes index.
    ISBN 1-59679-142-X (hardcover)
    ISBN 1-59679-143-8 (paperback)
        1. English language--Consonants--Juvenile literature. I. Title. II. Series.
    PE1159.S179 2005
    428.1'3--dc22
                                                                        2004059948

SandCastle™ books are created by a professional team of educators, reading specialists, and content developers around five essential components that include phonemic awareness, phonics, vocabulary, text comprehension, and fluency. All books are written, reviewed, and leveled for guided reading, early intervention reading, and Accelerated Reader® programs and designed for use in shared, guided, and independent reading and writing activities to support a balanced approach to literacy instruction.

Let Us Know

After reading the book, SandCastle would like you to tell us your stories about reading. What is your favorite page? Was there something hard that you needed help with? Share the ups and downs of learning to read. We want to hear from you! To get posted on the ABDO Publishing Company Web site, send us e-mail at:

sandcastle@abdopub.com

SandCastle Level: Beginning

dr

ABCDEFGH

IJKLMNOPQ

RSTUVWXYZ

abcdefgh

ijklmnopq

rstuvwxyz

Drew

Drake

drum

drink

dress

dragonfly

drill

The is red.

The is sweet.

Look at the .

The has wings.

Here is a .

Drew likes the drum.

Drake likes the dragonfly.

The dragonfly is on the drum.

Which of these pictures begin with **dr**?

More words that begin with dr

dragon

drapes

draw

dream

dresser

drive

drop

dry

About SandCastle™

A professional team of educators, reading specialists, and content developers created the SandCastle™ series to support young readers as they develop reading skills and strategies and increase their general knowledge. The SandCastle™ series has four levels that correspond to early literacy development in young children. The levels are provided to help teachers and parents select the appropriate books for young readers.

Emerging Readers
(no flags)

Beginning Readers
(1 flag)

Transitional Readers
(2 flags)

Fluent Readers
(3 flags)

These levels are meant only as a guide. All levels are subject to change.

ABDO
Publishing Company

To see a complete list of SandCastle™ books and other nonfiction titles from ABDO Publishing Company, visit www.abdopub.com or contact us at: 4940 Viking Drive, Edina, Minnesota 55435 • 1-800-800-1312 • fax: 1-952-831-1632